The Unstoppable Mary Seacole

Thuo Books

I am Mary Seacole. I was born in about 1805 in Kingston, on the sunny island of Jamaica in the Caribbean. My parents were from two very different cultures. My father was a British soldier from Scotland and my mother was a Jamaican doctress, who cared for sick people at the boarding house she owned.

I loved to watch my mother work and practised my own medical skills on my doll. I knew from an early age that I wanted to help people, just like my mother.

By the age of 12, I was allowed to help. I had a lot of practice caring for ill army officers and their wives.

When I was older, I decided to go to Panama and visit my brother. He owned a hotel there. At the time of my travels, parts of the railway were still being made and the sea crossing to Panama was not very safe but I was brave and decided to go anyway.

To my surprise, my brother's hotel was very busy as there were people coming through Panama in search of gold in California. On my first night there, I even had to sleep under the table as there were no free beds until the guests left in the morning.

There was a lot of illness in Panama and I helped as many people as I could to get better. I even set up my own restaurant. I got very good at running my own business.

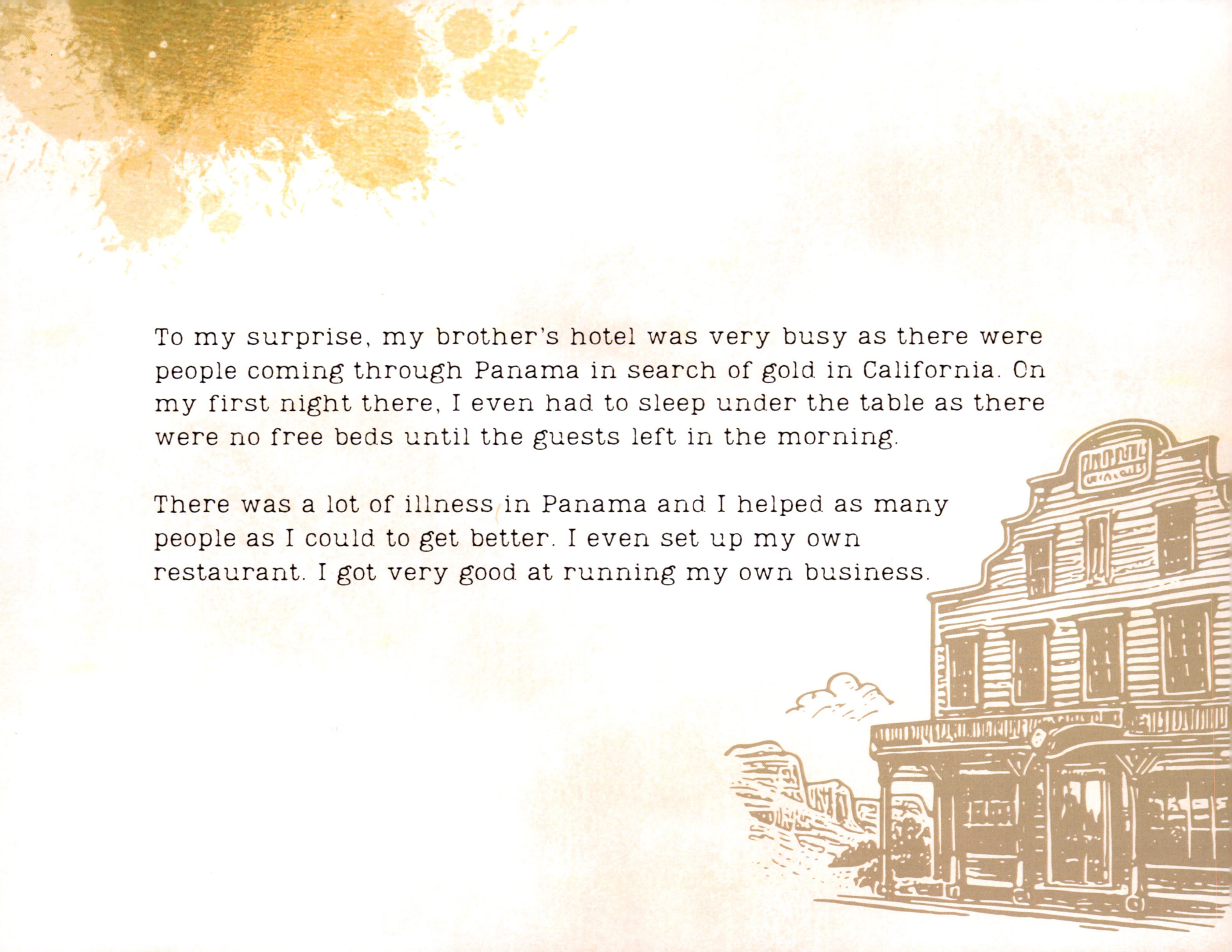

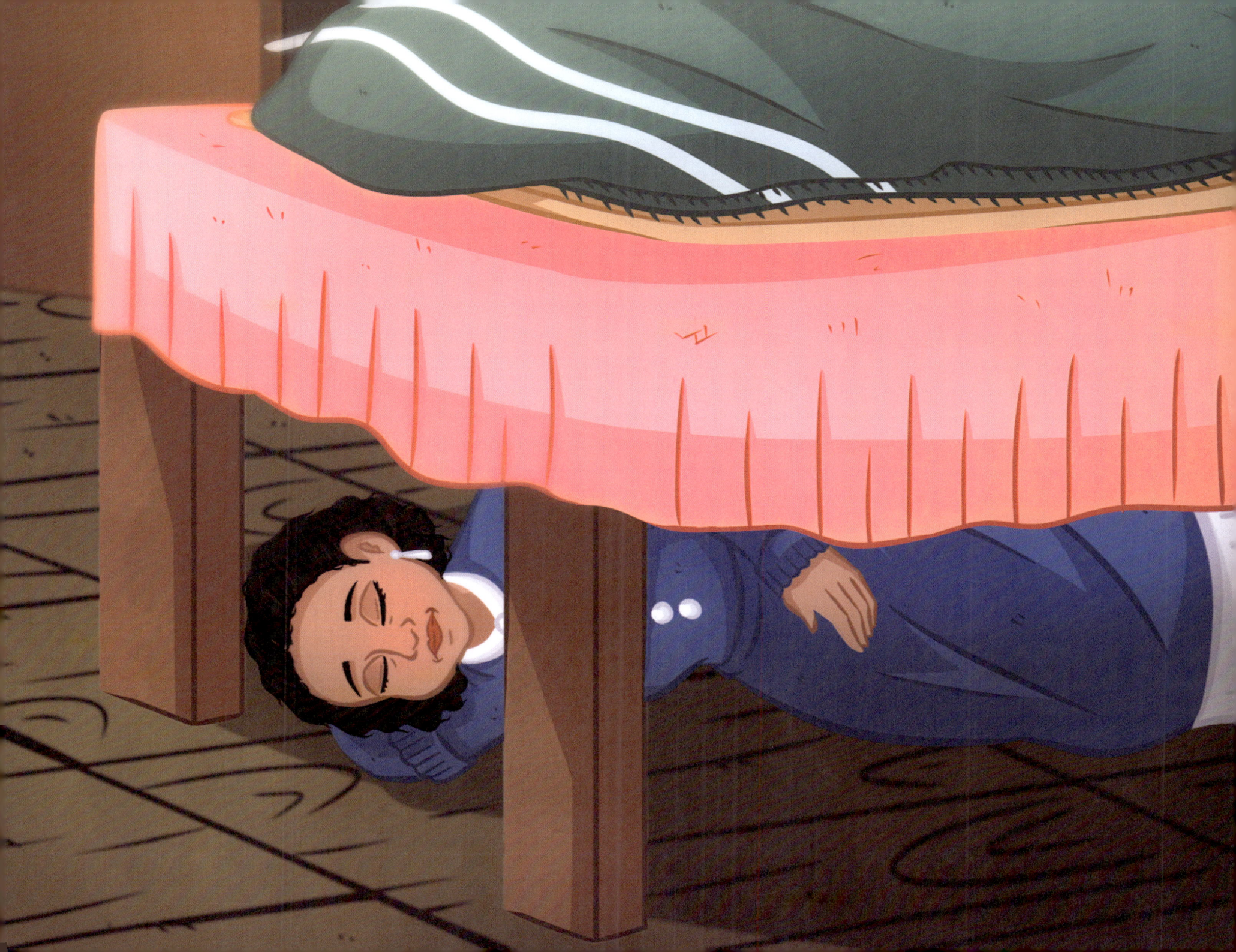

When returning to Kingston, I had a lot of trouble finding a boat that would take me, as the white American passengers did not want to travel with a woman of Black heritage. In the end, I had to get on a different boat.

However, I never let how other people felt about me stop me from doing what I set out to do and I soon wanted more adventures. I was keen to explore making money from the gold mining at a place called Escribanos. It was there that I met a very kind man called Thomas Day.

Even though I was very keen to make money from gold mining, when I heard there was war in the Crimea I longed to go and help nurse the soldiers, even though I was very far away. Some of the soldiers that had gone were ones I had already cared for in Jamaica.

I decided to go to England. While I was there, I offered my skills to Florence Nightingale's team, who were sending nurses to the Crimea. I knew the illnesses they had there were similar to ones I had treated in the past, and I knew I was more than able to treat the people there.

My time in England was not easy. I constantly tried to offer my help but felt no one wanted to listen. In the end, I knew why. People refused to look beyond my darker skin colour and they would not give me a chance to help. It wasn't fair.

I had come too far to be told no. I was determined to go. I paid my way there and, with the help of Thomas Day, who was also going to Crimea, we set up the British Hotel. This was a place to feed, heal, and provide supplies to soldiers fighting in the war.

From our hotel, which was much closer to the battlefield than the hospital, I was able to help. We sold little luxuries that people took for granted at home but were hard to find on the front line, like handkerchiefs. We also sold food to the soldiers, which helped to pay for building and running our hotel.

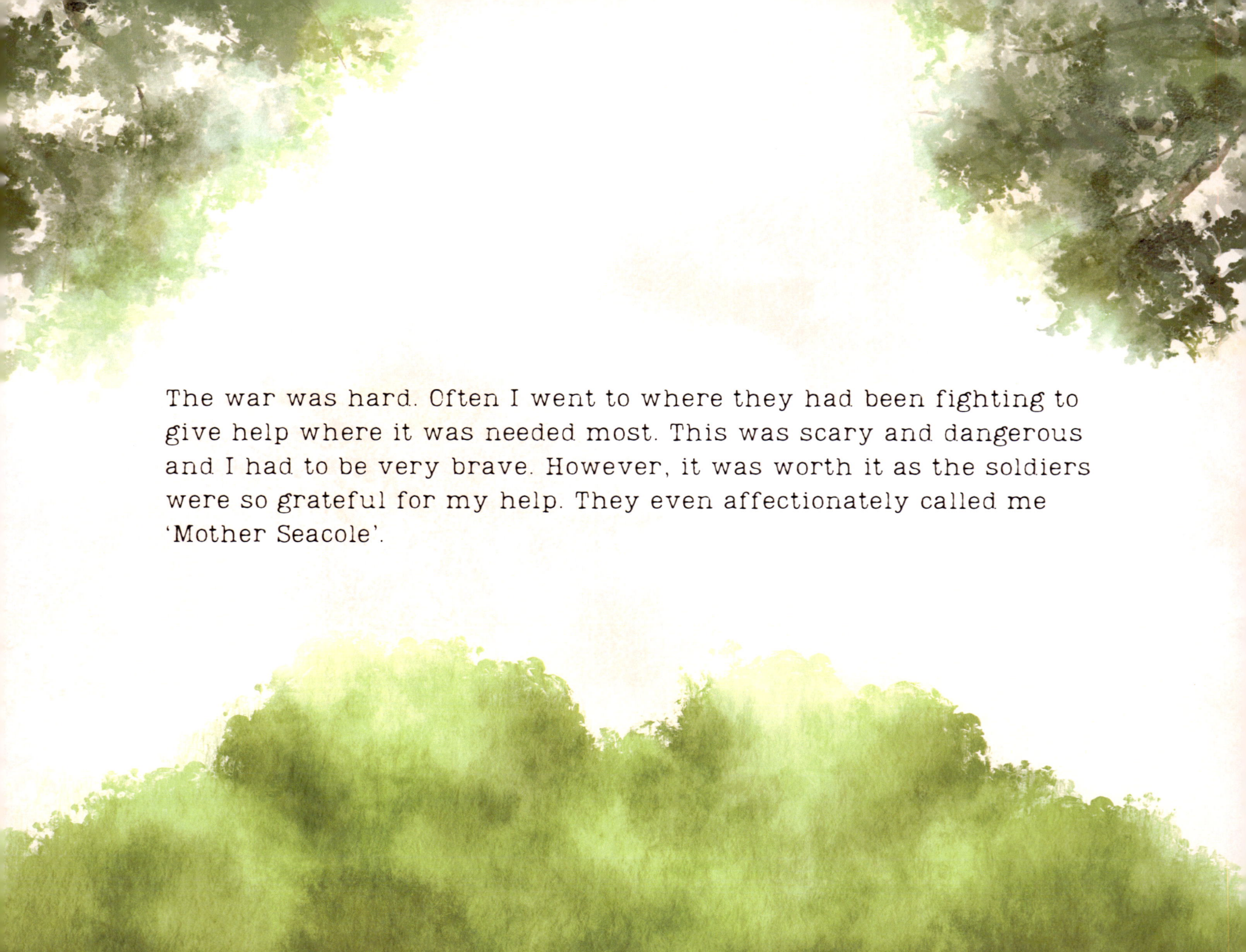

The war was hard. Often I went to where they had been fighting to give help where it was needed most. This was scary and dangerous and I had to be very brave. However, it was worth it as the soldiers were so grateful for my help. They even affectionately called me 'Mother Seacole'.

Finally, however, the fighting was over. There was much celebration at the British Hotel before everyone left for home.

~~British Hotel~~ closed

I tried miserably to sell the stock at the British Hotel that was left after all our customers had gone. There was no longer any need for the items I had to sell and I got barely anything in return for any of the stock or the building I had worked so hard to build. I returned to England with no money.

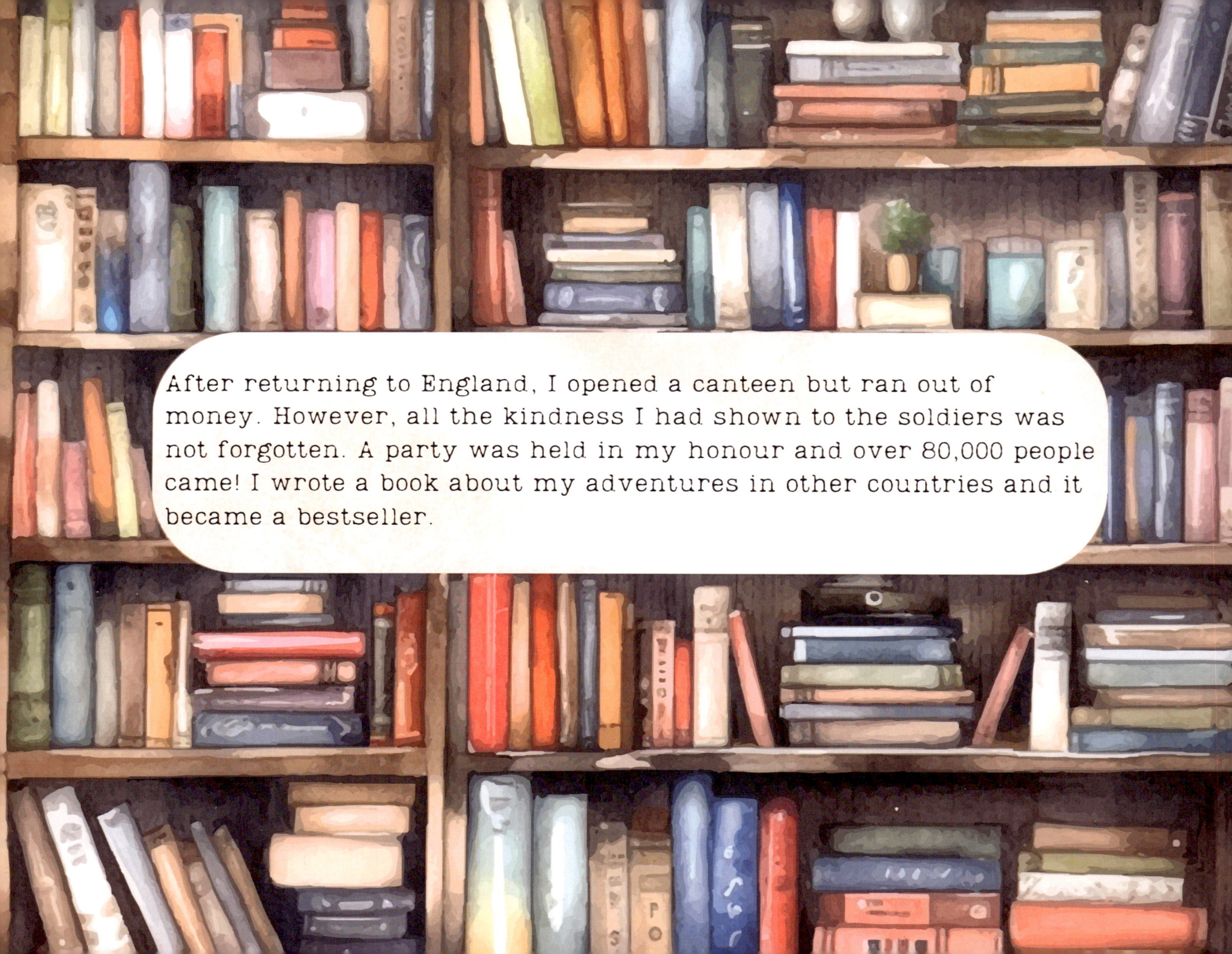

After returning to England, I opened a canteen but ran out of money. However, all the kindness I had shown to the soldiers was not forgotten. A party was held in my honour and over 80,000 people came! I wrote a book about my adventures in other countries and it became a bestseller.

To all those who face adversity, may they find the strength to persevere as Mary Seacole did.

Written and designed by Lucy Thuo
Main Illustrations by Eryanto

Other Images:
World map, Public domain

Copyright (c) Lucy Thuo, 2024
All rights reserved.

This book is based on Mary Seacole's autobiography, Wonderful Adventures of Mrs. Seacole in Many Lands, which was published in 1857.

No part of this book can be reproduced in any form or by written, electronic or mechanical, including photocopying, recording, or by any information retrieval system without written permission in writing by the author.

Published by Thuo Books

Although every precaution has been taken in the preparation of this book, the publisher and author assume no responsibility for errors or omissions. Neither is any liability assumed for damages resulting from the use of information contained herein.

ISBN: 978-1-917762-07-6

www.ingramcontent.com/pod-product-compliance
Lightning Source LLC
Chambersburg PA
CBRC102341090526
44590CB00010B/153